MY INFO

NAME:

NICKNAMES:

AGE:

THINGS I LIKE:

MY BEST MATES:

MY YOUTUBE NAME:

MY FAVOURITE YOUTUBERS:

WHY USE THIS BOOK?

Make your YouTube videos better!

Keep a record of your videos so you know which ones are the most popular.

Keep a record of the topics you cover so you can make sure you don't do the same thing each time.

Show your parents how being a YouTuber can be good for your education…
it teaches you planning and organising, writing and storytelling, innovation, technology skills, editing skills, how to think about your target audience, and how to be safe whilst using the internet. How could they refuse?

If you create epic videos and get lots of followers, you can start to make money!

ISBN: 978-1-912293-02-5

BEFORE YOU START:

Choose what type of YouTuber you want to be? Do you want to focus on gaming? Do you want to be a vlogger where you are the star of the show? Do you want to focus on doing product reviews where you show new toys or gadgets and review them? Do you want to show stunts and tricks or skills (such as cool hairstyles or sports skills)

What equipment will you use? Will you use a video-camera, a tablet or a camera phone, a webcam or an action camera like a GoPro? Will you use a tripod or a selfie-stick to keep the camera steady? What editing software have you got?

Have you set up a YouTube account? Choose your YouTube name. Not your real name, but something memorable. Decide on whether your YouTube channel will be private or public. If you are under 13 years old you will need your parents to set it up.

Don't forget SAFETY. Remember that everything shared on the Internet can me viewed by anybody - good or bad, kind or mean. Keep your personal information (real name, age, address, school) private. Agree with your parents if you are allowed to appear in your videos, or just a screen, or your hands, for example. Don't respond to any comments that are unkind. Report these to YouTube immediately and ignore them. Speak to your parents about how you will use YouTube safely.

SHHH! FILMING IN PROGRESS
AND OTHER HINTS AND TIPS ON HOW TO MAKE COOL VIDEOS

👍 Make a "Shhh! Filming in Progress" sign so you don't get interrupted by your parents or a brother or sister.

👍 Make sure you have good lighting.

👍 Make sure there isn't anything in the background you don't want people to see (like your messy bedroom or anything with personal information on it)

👍 Don't have long pauses in the commentary. Plan what you're going to say in advance or do a voice-over afterwards, or use music.

👍 Always have an opening phrase but think of ways to keep it fresh.

👍 Always use your YouTube name.

👍 Tell people what you're going to do in your video at the start and have a consistent ending.

👍 Remind viewers to like and comment and subscribe.

👍 Use editing software, like iMovie, to add music, time-lapse, slo-mo and voice-over.

👍 Plan your video so it's successful first time

NOW LET'S GET STARTED >

CONTENT BRAINSTORM

Think of all your favourite vlogs / youtube videos, or new ideas you've thought of. Use this space to write down all your ideas. You can come back to this space for inspiration when planning each of your new videos....

CONTENT BRAINSTORM

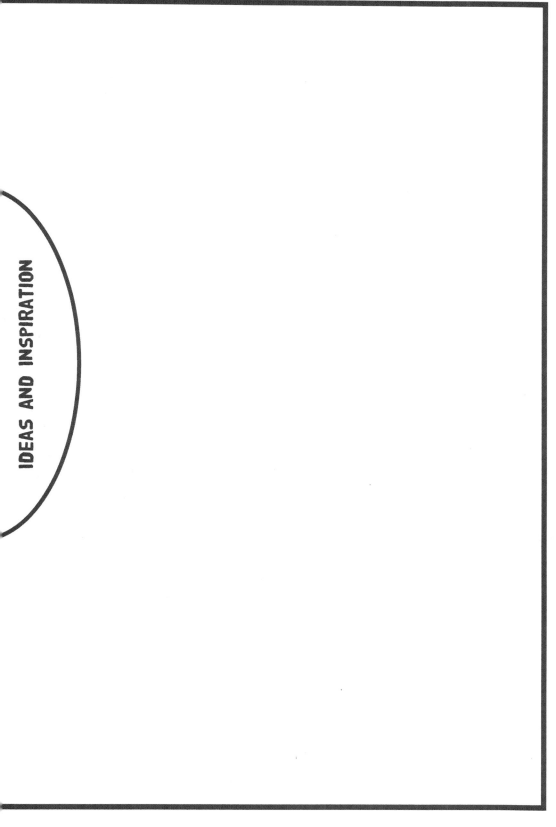

IDEAS AND INSPIRATION

PLAN NO. 1

Type of video (circle):
Vlog / Product Review / Gaming / Fun and Pranks /
Stunts and Skills

What is the topic of this video?

_____

_____

What will happen in this video?
How will it start? What will happen in the
middle? How will it end?

_____

_____

_____

_____

_____

_____

_____

What will the title be?

_____

Who will watch the video?
What will they like about it?

_____

_____

_____

_____

SuCCESS?

Video Statistics:

Date uploaded: _____

Views ____   👍 ____   👎 ____

Shares ____   Comments ____   Subscribers ____

How would YOU rate your video out of 10? _____

Would you do anything differently next time?

_____

_____

PLAN NO. 2

Type of video (circle):
Vlog / Product Review / Gaming / Fun and Pranks /
Stunts and Skills

What is the topic of this video?

_____

_____

What will happen in this video?
How will it start? What will happen in the
middle? How will it end?

_____

_____

_____

_____

_____

_____

_____

What will the title be?

_____

Who will watch the video?
What will they like about it?

_____

_____

_____

SuCCESS?

Video Statistics:

Date uploaded: _____

Views ___ 👍 ___ 👎 ___

Shares ___   Comments ___   Subscribers ___

How would YOU rate your video out of 10? _____

Would you do anything differently next time?

_____

_____

PLAN NO. 3

Type of video (circle):
Vlog / Product Review / Gaming / Fun and Pranks /
Stunts and Skills

What is the topic of this video?

_____

_____

What will happen in this video?
How will it start? What will happen in the
middle? How will it end?

_____

_____

_____

_____

_____

_____

_____

What will the title be?

_____

Who will watch the video?
What will they like about it?

_____

_____

_____

SUCCESS?

Video Statistics:

Date uploaded: _____

Views ___   👍 ___   👎 ___

Shares ___   Comments ___   Subscribers ___

How would YOU rate your video out of 10? _____

Would you do anything differently next time?

_____

_____

PLAN NO. 4

Type of video (circle):
Vlog / Product Review / Gaming / Fun and Pranks /
Stunts and Skills

What is the topic of this video?

_____

_____

What will happen in this video?
How will it start? What will happen in the
middle? How will it end?

_____

_____

_____

_____

_____

_____

_____

What will the title be?

_____

Who will watch the video?
What will they like about it?

_____

_____

_____

_____

SuCCESS?

Video Statistics:

Date uploaded: _____

Views ____

Shares ____   Comments ____   Subscribers ____

How would YOU rate your video out of 10? _____

Would you do anything differently next time?

_____

_____

PLAN NO. 5

Type of video (circle):
Vlog / Product Review / Gaming / Fun and Pranks /
Stunts and Skills

What is the topic of this video?

_____

_____

What will happen in this video?
How will it start? What will happen in the
middle? How will it end?

_____

_____

_____

_____

_____

_____

_____

What will the title be?

_____

Who will watch the video?
What will they like about it?

_____

_____

_____

_____

SUCCESS?

Video Statistics:

Date uploaded: _____

Views ____   👍 ____   👎 ____

Shares ____   Comments ____   Subscribers ____

How would YOU rate your video out of 10? _____

Would you do anything differently next time?

_____

_____

PLAN NO. 6

Type of video (circle):
Vlog / Product Review / Gaming / Fun and Pranks /
Stunts and Skills

What is the topic of this video?

_____

_____

What will happen in this video?
How will it start? What will happen in the
middle? How will it end?

_____

_____

_____

_____

_____

_____

_____

What will the title be?

_____

Who will watch the video?
What will they like about it?

_____

_____

_____

SUCCESS?

Video Statistics:

Date uploaded: _____

Views ___   👍 ___   👎 ___

Shares ___   Comments ___   Subscribers ___

How would YOU rate your video out of 10? _____

Would you do anything differently next time?

_____

_____

PLAN NO. 7

Type of video (circle):
Vlog / Product Review / Gaming / Fun and Pranks /
Stunts and Skills

What is the topic of this video?

_____

_____

What will happen in this video?
How will it start? What will happen in the
middle? How will it end?

_____

_____

_____

_____

_____

_____

_____

What will the title be?

_____

Who will watch the video?
What will they like about it?

_____

_____

_____

_____

SuCCESS?

Video Statistics:

Date uploaded: _____

Views ____   👍 ____   👎 ____

Shares ____   Comments ____   Subscribers ____

How would YOU rate your video out of 10? _____

Would you do anything differently next time?

_____

_____

PLAN NO. 8

Type of video (circle):
Vlog / Product Review / Gaming / Fun and Pranks /
Stunts and Skills

What is the topic of this video?

_____

_____

What will happen in this video?
How will it start? What will happen in the
middle? How will it end?

_____

_____

_____

_____

_____

_____

_____

What will the title be?

_____

Who will watch the video?
What will they like about it?

_____

_____

_____

SuCCESS?

Video Statistics:

Date uploaded: _____

Views ____   👍 ____   👎 ____

Shares ____   Comments ____   Subscribers ____

How would YOU rate your video out of 10? _____

Would you do anything differently next time?

_____

_____

PLAN NO. 9

Type of video (circle):
Vlog / Product Review / Gaming / Fun and Pranks /
Stunts and Skills

What is the topic of this video?

_____

_____

What will happen in this video?
How will it start? What will happen in the
middle? How will it end?

_____

_____

_____

_____

_____

_____

_____

_____

What will the title be?

_____

Who will watch the video?
What will they like about it?

_____

_____

_____

_____

SUCCESS?

Video Statistics:

Date uploaded: _____

Views ____   👍 ____   👎 ____

Shares ____   Comments ____   Subscribers ____

How would YOU rate your video out of 10? _____

Would you do anything differently next time?

_____

_____

PLAN NO. 10

Type of video (circle):
Vlog / Product Review / Gaming / Fun and Pranks /
Stunts and Skills

What is the topic of this video?

_____

_____

What will happen in this video?
How will it start? What will happen in the
middle? How will it end?

_____

_____

_____

_____

_____

_____

_____

What will the title be?

_____

Who will watch the video?
What will they like about it?

_____

_____

_____

SUCCESS?

Video Statistics:

Date uploaded: _____

Views ___   👍 ___   👎 ___

Shares ___   Comments ___   Subscribers ___

How would YOU rate your video out of 10? _____

Would you do anything differently next time?

_____

_____

INDEX

Keep track of all your videos here...

Date	Video Title	Duration	Views / Likes / Comments / Shares
e.g. 02/07/17	Fidget Spinner Spin-Off	2m31s	14 Views, 10 Likes, 1 Comment, 0 Shares

Date	Video Title	Duration	Views / Likes / Comments / Shares

NOTES

_____

_____

_____

_____

_____

_____

_____

_____

NEED MORE PAGES ?

Check out www.amazon.co.uk for further volumes.

Made in the USA
Lexington, KY
11 January 2019